LORD
TEACH US
TO PRAY

Finding a Deeper Relationship
with Our Father

LYNN WISE

Blessed be the God and Father of our Lord Jesus Christ,

who has blessed us with every spiritual blessing

in the heavenly places in Christ.

—EPHESIANS 1:3

It is such an honor and blessing to study God's Word. Without Him first teaching me, I would have absolutely nothing to say. Therefore, I dedicate this study back to God. My prayer is that the following words bring Him glory and honor as they draw us closer to Him. Praise Him!

I would also like to dedicate this study to my grandchildren, Fisher, Olivia Hart, and Cooper. They bring joy to my life and inspire me to finish well. It is my prayer that my life will honor Christ and point my grandchildren to Him. I love them so dearly and want to see them grow to know and love the Lord.

TABLE OF CONTENTS

PREFACE

Are you "in a relationship"? That question brings a sweet warmth to some hearts and strikes terrifying fear in others. It has a distinct implication of connection, trust, and commitment. Whether you are speaking of a friendship, a kinship, or a soulmate, each relationship is individually unique. What works for one relationship may not be the best for another. The basics are solid and much the same, but the peripherals can be just as diverse as the people involved can.

Are you "in a relationship" with God? What is your connection to Him? How much do you trust Him? What is your commitment to Him? Do these questions catch you off guard? Have you ever considered the dynamics of your relationship with the Creator of the universe? If not, you are in the right place! That's exactly what we are here to accomplish!

Communication is the foundation of all relationships. They cannot be built without communication, which is vital for the relationship to remain strong and healthy. In this study, we will cultivate our individual and unique relationships with God by strengthening our communication with Him. Our connections will grow stronger as we deepen our trust in Him. True commitment is sure to follow as our relationships begins to flourish.

I am so thankful you have decided to study with me! I promise that God's Word will not let you down. My prayer is that through these pages you get to know the God of the universe as never before, filling your heart with an insatiable desire to nurture your relationship with Him each day.

Blessings!

Lynn Wise

SECTION 1:

LIVING IN RELATIONSHIP

How many relationships do you currently have? I suspect that your guess would be too low. With how many family members do you have a relationship? How many friends? How many coworkers? How many mentors? Mentees? Yes, that's a word.

On a scale of one to ten, these relationships vary in depth. Your relationship with your best friend is very different from your relationship with the barista at your local coffee shop. The barista may see you several times each week, but the relationship revolves around your favorite caffeine.

How about your relationship with God? What is the depth of that relationship? How often do you meet with Him for a conversation? How much time do you spend speaking with Him? And how much time do you spend listening to Him? We begin our relationship with God when we accept Jesus Christ as our Savior, but that is not the extent of the relationship. It's only the beginning. Our relationship with God takes time and investment. It takes conversation, which is prayer. It also takes listening—first by reading His Word and then by being still as we wait for His direction through the Holy Spirit.

> There is a difference in prayers of the Old and the New Testaments. As Habakkuk exemplifies, Old Testament prayer is based on the character of God and appeals to God's great mercies (Habakkuk 3). In the New Testament, prayer is based on a relationship with God through Jesus Christ. "When you pray, say: Our Father" (LUKE 11:2).[1]
>
> —OSWALD CHAMBERS

Jesus stands in the gap between the mercy of the Old Testament and the grace of the New Testament. He changed the dynamics, bringing God into sweet, tender relationship with His children. God is still God and we are still not, but we have moved past mercy (not getting what we deserve) into God's grace (receiving what we don't deserve), all because of this wonderful relationship with our Redeemer.

In this section, we will start to unfold our glorious relationship with the God of heaven. I cannot wait to explore Scripture with you!

Blessings!

LESSON 1

Our Desire

At a planning session for a women's ministry event at my home church, I closed the session by asking each of the eight women in attendance to join in a circle of prayer. We held hands as each woman, one by one, petitioned the Lord regarding the coming event. The power of the Holy Spirit surging through that prayer circle was undeniable as God's children reverently opened their hearts to Him.

Prayer, or speaking to the Creator, is a special privilege granted to every one of God's children. It has long been the desire of humankind to connect with God on a deeper level, and we may do so through this open line of communication

The Bible gives us access to many of David's conversations with God. His prayers are the cries of his heart. Here are a couple of examples where David expressed his deep desire to connect with God.

> **As the deer pants for the water brooks, so pants my soul for You, O God.**
>
> — PSALM 42:1

> **O God, You are my God; early will I seek You; my soul thirsts for You; my flesh longs for You in a dry and thirsty land where there is no water.**
>
> — PSALM 63:1

In a country where we take fresh water for granted, it may be hard to imagine a thirst so deep. Water is an interesting metaphor because we cannot live long without it. God is as much a necessity in our lives as water. Without Him, we perish.

How would you describe your desire for God?

Is He a necessity?

David's words paint the picture of an unquenchable thirst. It is true; we will never get enough of God. The more we spend time with Him, the more we want to spend time with Him. We will never say, "My thirst is quenched. I'm full. I need no more."

However, we can feel a temporary quench when we spend time with Him. While in His presence, we can feel fullness like no other. We can feel the delicate touch of the Comforter. We can trust a faithful Friend. We can feel the protection of a fierce King. We can feel the unfailing love of a faithful Father. That, I believe, is what we all desire. God can and will fill all these necessities in our life.

What is your unquenchable thirst today? What is your most pressing need that only God can fill?

Jesus's disciples also felt the unquenchable thirst for the Lord. Let's join them in what was undoubtedly a life altering experience as they witnessed the very Son of God in intimate conversation with His Father.

> **Now it came to pass, as He was praying in a certain place, when He ceased, that one of His disciples said to Him, "Lord, teach us to pray, as John also taught his disciples."**
>
> — LUKE 11:1

Can you imagine hearing Jesus speak to His Father through prayer? How sweet yet powerful that conversation must have been. We don't know the content of the prayer, but we do know that it awakened a desire in the disciples. Jesus led by example and inspired them to desire more.

The disciples were no doubt on holy ground as Father and Son connected. Can you visualize the scene with me? The disciples likely also bowed their heads as they saw Jesus assume a position of submission. Tears must have streamed down their cheeks as they listened to Jesus's reverent, tender conversation with His Father. The disciples surely desired the intimacy that was evident in the words of Jesus, Son of God.

What would have been your reaction to hearing Jesus pray to His Father?

When Jesus ended the conversation with His Father, one of His disciples respectfully asked Him to teach them how to pray. It was their desire to connect with the Father with the same intimacy that Jesus had.

So He said to them, "When you pray, say:

Our Father in heaven."

—LUKE 11:2A

Without delay, Jesus taught them. He gave them the model prayer that is the blueprint for us all to quench our desire for an intimate relationship with our heavenly Father. It is possible for each of us to have that relationship. All we must do is ask Him to teach us. Then listen. I hope this lesson leaves you desiring more. Until tomorrow, stay thirsty!

Blessings!

PRAYER: Thank your heavenly Father for the unquenchable desire to know Him more.

LESSON 2

Our Positioning

My grandchildren and I love to play Chinese checkers. I am teaching them to position their marbles in a way that allows them to jump repeatedly across the board and win the game. As in many games, proper positioning is very important.

When the disciples asked Jesus to teach them how to pray, He responded by giving them a model for prayer. This is not a repetitious dialogue to be memorized and repeated without thought. It is a pattern that, when followed reverently, will position us for open communication with the King of glory.

In order to fully understand our position, we must first understand God's position in this relationship. Jesus solidified God's position by beginning His illustration with the proper salutation.

> **So He said to them, "When you pray, say: Our Father in heaven."**
>
> —LUKE 11:2A

We frequently start a conversation by addressing the person we are speaking to by name. In the same way, Jesus began by teaching us to address God as "Our Father in heaven."

Perhaps the first notation of position we see is heaven. God reigns over creation seated on His throne in heaven. This distinction helps us understand the distance between God's position and ours. He reigns high above us in heaven while we reside down here on earth.

The second position we see is that of Father. God is our heavenly Father. We hold the position of His child. While the first positioning involves physical location, this positioning is more complex because it involves relationship. In order to fully understand our position, we must understand the basis of the relationship.

Describe what it means to you to be a child of God.

If you have attended church for a long time, perhaps you know the scriptures called the "Romans Road" by heart and can recite them without really thinking about their meaning. I encourage you to read them with fresh eyes, relating each passage to your position in Christ and your position with the Father. If they are new to you, drink them in. Let what Christ has done for you soak into your heart.

Please begin by reading **Romans 3:23.**

> For all have sinned and fall short of the glory of God.
> —ROMANS 3:23

Like a great deal of the New Testament, the book of Romans was written by Paul. He was the self-proclaimed chief of sinners, yet he understood and joined the mission of Jesus Christ.

> This is a faithful saying and worthy of all acceptance, that Christ Jesus came into the world to save sinners, of whom I am chief.
> —1 TIMOTHY 1:15

We are all sinners by nature and by choice. Because of Adam's sin, we all have a sin nature, and we cannot overcome it on our own. **Romans 3:10** tells us no one is righteous. Not you. Not me. Not the best person we know. Only Christ Jesus.

> As it is written: "There is none righteous, no, not one."
> —ROMANS 3:10

Now that we understand our condition, please read **Romans 6:23** to discover our destination without Christ. Because of our sin, we all deserve death. It's plain and simple. But eternal life, the result of God's love for us, is a gift. The gift is free to us because it was bought with the sacrifice of Jesus on the cross.

> For the wages of sin is death, but the gift of God is eternal life in Christ Jesus our Lord.
> —ROMANS 6:23

As we read **Romans 5:8**, let the depth of God's love for you sink in. God loves us so much that He gave His one and only Son as a sacrifice to pay our sin debt once and for all. The sacrifice of God's Son on the cross is what sets us free from death and opens the door to eternal life. We have no ability to pay that debt, but the perfect Lamb of God is able.

> But God demonstrates His own love toward us, in that while we were still sinners, Christ died for us.
> —ROMANS 5:8

Our situation is clear. We are lost and undone without Christ. Praise God, **Romans 10:9–10** clearly shows that eternal life is waiting when we surrender to Jesus as our Lord. It's really that simple.

1. Admit you are a sinner.

2. Believe Jesus Christ is the Son of God. He lived a sinless life, was crucified for our sins, and God raised Him from the dead. Jesus now sits at the right hand of the Father interceding for us.

3. Confess Him as Lord and you become a child of God. **Romans 10:13** tells us, "Whoever calls on the name of the LORD shall be saved." No questions. No test to pass. Jesus paid it all. We owe our lives and our futures in eternity to Him. His sacrifice washed us white as snow. Our position is sealed. We can address God as our Father!

If you confess with your mouth the Lord Jesus and believe in your heart that God has raised Him from the dead, you will be saved. For with the heart one believes unto righteousness, and with the mouth confession is made unto salvation. For the Scripture says, "Whoever believes on Him will not be put to shame." For there is no distinction between Jew and Greek, for the same Lord over all is rich to all who call upon Him. For whoever calls on the name of the LORD shall be saved.

—ROMANS 10:9–13

Write John 3:16 in the space below.

Now list all the words or phrases in this verse that you thank God for.

I pray this little walk down the well-known Roman Road has renewed your understanding of your position as a child of God. It has certainly renewed my appreciation for the sacrifice Christ made for me. I know you are thankful as well. Keeping our position fresh in our minds deepens our relationship with the Father and the Son, and it prepares us for reverent conversation with our Father in heaven. See you tomorrow!

Blessings!

PRAYER: If you have never accepted Christ as your Savior, I hope you will pray that prayer right now. Call upon His Name and you will be saved! When you have done so, thank God for your salvation and the privilege to call Him your Father.

LESSON 3

Our Community

Hello, Sister! I am so thankful I can address you as a sister! Whether you accepted Christ as your Savior moments ago or years ago, we are forever sisters in Christ! God is *our* Father.

We were created for relationship. God instituted the relationships of marriage and family. He blessed friendships as He taught us how to love our neighbors. It is no coincidence that when Jesus taught us to pray, He instructed us to include others.

So He said to them, "When you pray, say: Our Father in heaven."

——LUKE 11:2A

Jesus's model prayer is not addressed to *my* Father but to *our* Father. The only singular references in the Lord's Prayer refer to God. He is the one true and living God and none other even comes close. References to God's children in the prayer are always plural.

Starting our prayers with "my" can set the tone for selfishness. On the other hand, beginning with "our" prepares our minds to pray for the good of all. It is good to always remember, He is our Father and working things together for our good. That said, there are times when we go to our Father with intimate one-on-one conversation. It is in these precious, very private moments alone with the Master that we can address Him as "my Father" because of our individual relationship with Him.

In order to pray effectively for our brothers and sisters, we must first *know* them. We cannot be specific in our prayers unless we know a little about the other person. That knowledge takes commitment to our community of believers, the church. It requires relationships here on earth.

Christianity is not a solo activity. Christianity involves community and fellowship with other believers. Much of the New Testament describes the establishment of the church and how we should conduct ourselves as the body of Christ. Let's see how Matthew encourages us on this subject of prayer.

Please read **Matthew 18:19–20**.

Three actions are listed.

What are they?

1.

2.

3.

> Again I say to you that if two of you agree on earth concerning anything that they ask, it will be done for them by My Father in heaven. For where two or three are gathered together in My name, I am there in the midst of them.
>
> —MATTHEW 18:19–20

Not only are we encouraged to gather together, we should also pray together in Jesus's name. That means agreeing with each other and agreeing with Christ on the matter. Paul took things a little further.

> Now may the God who gives endurance and encouragement allow you to live in harmony with one another, according to the command of Christ Jesus, so that you may glorify the God and Father of our Lord Jesus Christ with a united mind and voice.
>
> —ROMANS 15:5–6 (HCSB)

What does God give us that allows us to live in harmony?

How can we use these gifts to promote unity in our community of believers?

How does a united mind and voice glorify God?

In his letter to the church at Philippi, Paul touched again on like-mindedness and the sense of community that we find in a local church.

> Therefore if there is any consolation in Christ, if any comfort of love, if any fellowship of the Spirit, if any affection and mercy, fulfill my joy by being like-minded, having the same love, being of one accord, of one mind. Let nothing be done through selfish ambition or conceit, but in lowliness of mind let each esteem others better than himself. Let each of you look out not only for his own interests, but also for the interests of others.

—PHILIPPIANS 2:1–4

Our church family is just that, a family. We love one another. We look out for one another. We pray for one another. We worship with one another. We laugh together and we cry together. Our church families should be near and dear to our hearts.

By starting a prayer with "our," we acknowledge that we are one with the body of Christ. We are here to worship, honor, and adore our Father. And when we speak to Him, it is from a state of like-minded commitment to His Son, Jesus Christ.

How would you describe your current commitment to your church family?

If you are not a member of a local church, I encourage you to find a group of like-minded believers and join them. Worship our Lord with your brothers and sisters. Fellowship with God's children is a sweet relationship like no other. It's His desire and it brings Him glory.

Blessings!

PRAYER: Thank God for your church family.

LESSON 4

Our Reverence

I'm going to show my age a bit here by admitting that I grew up in a generation where children were taught to respect those who were older and in authority. "Yes, ma'am" and "yes, sir" were common and expected parts of my vocabulary.

Sadly, the world today has lost much of its value for respect, but the fact remains that our heavenly Father still deserves and demands it. In the model prayer, Jesus immediately followed His greeting with reverence.

> **Hallowed be Your name.**
>
> —LUKE 11:2B

The Holman Christian Standard Bible translates the word *hallowed* as "Your name be honored as holy." To have true relationship with the Creator of the universe, we must humbly reverence His name. He is not "the man upstairs." He is not a casual acquaintance. His name is not a slang term as some may use it. He is the Ruler of all. How do we define "all"? Everything in the universe. He created and is Ruler of all—the King of kings and Lord of lords. His name is hallowed, sacred, and holy. He is Deity. His name should be spoken reverently as we humble ourselves in His holy presence and seek conversation. David said it this way:

> **O Lord, our Lord, How excellent is Your name in all the earth,**
> **who have set Your glory above the heavens!**
>
> —PSALM 8:1

How would you describe the holiness of God's name?

When we begin to understand the holiness of God, our reverence will not lag far behind. For a few moments, let's look at how a few people in Scripture reverenced God.

Please read the reference, and then describe how the writer respected God the Father or God the Son.

David   PSALM 51:1–4

_____

Isaiah   ISAIAH 6:1–8

_____

John the
Baptist   MARK 1:1–8

_____

Mary   LUKE 1:26–38

_____

Joseph   MATTHEW 1:18–25

What about you? How is your reverence for our Father evident?

When we fully see God for Who He is, we cannot help feeling as Isaiah did and with bowed head say, "Woe is me." But like Isaiah, our sin has been purged. Not by a hot coal but by the very blood of Christ Jesus! Because of Christ, we can raise our face to heaven and say, "Here I am, send me!" Our God is awesome and so very worthy of our reverence.

Blessings!

PRAYER: Thank God for His majesty and the privilege to reverently speak His holy name.

SECTION 2:

LIVING IN SUBMISSION

While learning to drive, and hopefully before we ever get behind the wheel, we must first learn the rules of the road. Among other things, we learn the meaning of all the road signs. One very important sign tells us to "yield." It means we must yield the right of way to oncoming traffic. Anyone in the main flow of traffic gets to go first. We must slow down, let them proceed, and then fall in behind them without hindering the main flow.

Living in submission to God is somewhat like living in the yield lane. God's will is always the main flow, and we should always yield to His will and fall in behind Him. We never want to be found hindering the flow of the will of God. In fact, we should desire to be actively used by God to accomplish His will.

> It has well been said that the purpose of prayer is not to get man's will done in heaven, but to get God's will done on earth. Prayer is not telling God what we want and then selfishly enjoying it. Prayer is asking God to use us to accomplish what He wants so that His name is glorified. His kingdom is extended and strengthened, and

His will is done. I must test all of my personal requests by these overruling concerns if I expect God to hear and answer my prayers.[1]

—WARREN W. WIERSBE

It is fitting that reverence precedes Jesus's instruction on yielding. In order to yield, we must submit control. We will never fully submit unless we fully respect and trust the One we are submitting to. Submission without relationship is simply bondage, while submission within a relationship demonstrates reverence, honor, and love. It all works perfectly together.

In this section, we will understand what it means to live in submission to God's will. I cannot wait to yield to the God of heaven alongside you!

Blessings!

LESSON 5

Your Kingdom

Countless people are fascinated by the monarchy of England. After all, what little girl never pretended to be a princess? Or better yet, the queen! Greater than any earthly kingdom with its human ruler is God's kingdom, ruled by the King of glory. In God's kingdom, He rules and reigns as King for eternity. There is no other authority. He is the sovereign Ruler. So, what does it mean when Jesus teaches us to pray for the following?

> **Your kingdom come.**
>
> —LUKE 11:2C

This request first acknowledges that the kingdom unquestionably belongs to God. It's His and His alone. By praying this, we acknowledge that the kingdom we desire is a place where all submit to the one true and living God.

When you think of God's kingdom, what comes to mind for you? Describe what you see in your mind's eye.

If we look closely, we see a dual meaning in this request for God's kingdom to come. The key to the duality is, come where? When I first think of the kingdom of God, my mind turns to heaven. God is certainly Ruler in His heavenly kingdom. When we pray "Your kingdom come," we are asking Jesus, as John did in his revelation, to return to this earth as King in His second coming.

> **He who testifies to these things says, "Surely I am coming quickly." Amen. Even so, come, Lord Jesus!**
>
> —REVELATION 22:20

As we await the second coming of Christ, we have a responsibility. Waiting in submission requires action. Between Jesus's resurrection and ascension, He gave us the great commission.

> **And Jesus came and spoke to them, saying, "All authority has been given to Me in heaven and on earth. Go therefore and make disciples of all the nations, baptizing them in the name of the Father and of the Son and of the Holy Spirit, teaching them to observe all things that I have commanded you; and lo, I am with you always, even to the end of the age." Amen.**
>
> —MATTHEW 28:18–20

Jesus gave us two distinct directives—lead people to Christ and teach them to obey His commands. We should be doing this work until Jesus returns.

So, when Jesus tells us to pray for His return, a burning question comes to mind. Are we finished with His assignment? Have we exhausted our resources to introduce everyone we encounter to Christ? Have we effectively discipled those around us and taught them His commands? Will the Lord say to us, "Well done, good and faithful servant" (Matthew 5:21)? When He returns, our opportunity to make disciples will be over.

> **For if we believe that Jesus died and rose again, even so God will bring with Him those who sleep in Jesus. For this we say to you by the word of the Lord, that we who are alive and remain**

until the coming of the Lord will by no means precede those who are asleep. For the Lord Himself will descend from heaven with a shout, with the voice of an archangel, and with the trumpet of God. And the dead in Christ will rise first. Then we who are alive and remain shall be caught up together with them in the clouds to meet the Lord in the air. And thus we shall always be with the Lord.

—1 THESSALONIANS 4:14–17

This is a glorious day for those who know Christ as Savior. However, for the lost it means damnation, for their chance to know Christ has past.

Who in your circle of influence does not know Christ as their Savior?

Have you done all you can do to introduce them to Christ?

Before we can passionately pray for Jesus's return, we should make sure that we are completing our work well. Two of the most difficult conversations to have with someone who does not share our opinions involve politics and religion. Are we personally capable of changing someone's beliefs? We are not, but God made a way. This is what happens when we accept Christ as our Savior.

You shall receive power when the Holy Spirit has come upon you; and you shall be witnesses to Me in Jerusalem, and in all Judea and Samaria, and to the end of the earth.

—ACTS 1:8

This leads to the second meaning of asking God's kingdom to come. We are asking God to be King and Ruler of our lives. Although we receive the Holy Spirit when we are saved, we must submit to God and allow Him to control our lives every moment of every day. How can we do that?

> **Rejoice always, pray without ceasing, in everything give thanks; for this is the will of God in Christ Jesus for you. Do not quench the Spirit. Do not despise prophecies. Test all things; hold fast what is good. Abstain from every form of evil.**

> —1 THESSALONIANS 5:16–22

We must submit to the leadership of the Holy Spirit and let His power work in and through us. We must get to know Him and allow Him to be the dominant influence in our lives. He alone has the power to change minds for Christ.

When we submit to the Holy Spirit and give Him control, something awesome happens. Our relationship with Jesus progresses from knowing Him as Savior to knowing Him as King and Lord. Our hearts and lives become His kingdom and His reign is supreme. When the Holy Spirit is in control, we willingly and lovingly live in submission to His will.

I want to pause a moment to take inventory of our level of submission in our relationships with God. Take your time. Pray about each area and respond honestly before God. I will start by listing a few areas of life we all share.

Please rate your level of submission in each area by placing an "X" in the column that best describes your level of submission to God. Then add other areas at the bottom that you feel are important.

Area	I am in control.	I am trying to give God control.	I am fully submitted to God.
My Friendships			
My Free Time			
My Tithes and Offerings			

It is my prayer that this exercise gives us encouragement and sparks resolve in our hearts to fully submit to the Holy Spirit in all areas of our lives. Don't be discouraged if you aren't there yet. Regardless of what others may think or say, no one is perfect. We, like Paul, are all pressing toward the goal for the prize of the upward call of God in Christ Jesus. Forget what is behind you. Reach forward to what lies ahead. Press on, my friend! Press on!

Blessings!

PRAYER: Thank God for His kingdom, your heavenly home. Invite Him, through the Holy Spirit, to be Ruler of your heart in every area of your life.

LESSON 6

Your Will

The phrase "Where there's a will, there's a way" is the modern version of an old English proverb.[1] Today the phrase is used to imply that if a person has the desire and determination to get something done, they will find a way to accomplish it. This phrase is near and dear to me, as I am sure it is others. I am at heart a country girl with a great deal of grit. If I want to do something, I can usually figure out how. This mindset of self-reliance can become a great hindrance when we dig into the next line of the model prayer.

> **Your will be done.**
>
> —LUKE 11:2D

When we ladies with grit cannot fulfill our desires, we sometimes ask God to help us accomplish our will with little regard for how it lines up with His will. Instead, we independent ladies must learn how to yield to our Father's will.

What are you asking of God that is your will? Explain.

To him that will, waies are not wanting.[2]

—UNKNOWN AUTHOR

The oldest version of the "will and way" phrase originates back in 1640. Isn't that also true of God? There are countless examples in the Bible where God used men and women to accomplish His will. He also used a great fish, several donkeys, and an old rugged cross. When Jesus was asked to rebuke his followers for rejoicing at His triumphant entry into Jerusalem, He said that if they were silenced, the stones would cry out (see Luke 19:40). God's ways to accomplish His will are certainly not wanting.

By requesting that God's will be done, we are not just passively submitting to it. We are not meant to sit on the sidelines and watch God's will play out. We are agreeing that God's will is best and requesting the privilege to be a part of accomplishing it. Requesting that God's will be done both denies our fleshly will and commits us to playing an active part in His perfect will. It expresses trust. We make a conscious decision to seek and know His will and then pursue it. When that happens, God's will can be accomplished in and through us. Learning to submit to God's will is an important milestone in our relationship with Him.

How do we know God's will? It's actually very simple. We learn the desires of God the same way we learn the desires of others we are close to. We listen to Him. The Bible is God's love letter to us. When we open His Word, we will hear His voice.

> **All Scripture is inspired by God and is useful to teach us what is true and to make us realize what is wrong in our lives. It corrects us when we are wrong and teaches us to do what is right. God uses it to prepare and equip his people to do every good work.**

> —2 TIMOTHY 3:16–17 (NLT)

The Bible is the living Word of God. It is God-breathed. When we read it and meditate on it, we will hear Him speak to us. His Word will convict us of our inadequacies. We will receive training from the Master. God's Word,

His promises and principles, should in turn motivate our prayers. The voice of God, through His Word, will never direct us outside the will of God. When we allow God to speak to us through His Word, we begin to change. Our will transforms to align with His will.

> I beseech you therefore, brethren, by the mercies of God, that you present your bodies a living sacrifice, holy, acceptable to God, which is your reasonable service. And do not be conformed to this world, but be transformed by the renewing of your mind, that you may prove what is that good and acceptable and perfect will of God.
>
> —ROMANS 12:1–2

God is in the transforming business. As we read His Word, mediate on it, and let it flood our hearts, our minds will be transformed. As we submit ourselves to God as a living sacrifice, we will begin to see things from God's perspective and desire His will over our own.

When we fully connect in relationship with our heavenly Father, we change. We begin to see His will and His way so that we understand His direction for our lives. At times, His will does align with our human desires. But without our submitting to His will in fervent and reverent prayer, would we recognize it as God's will and work?

Take the prayer you noted at the beginning of this lesson and transform it into a prayer asking for God's will in the matter.

If you have trouble doing this, open God's Word. Use a Bible app or a website to search Scripture for words or phrases that relate to your need. See what His Word has to say about it. Pray for God to show you His will in the matter. Then have another try.

Blessings!

PRAYER: Thank God for His Holy Word. Submit to Him by asking Him to transform your mind to His perfect will.

LESSON 7

Your Will, Your Way

It is commonly said that the shortest distance between two points is a straight line. I respect that. Being direct and concise is the fastest way to a solution. However, in matters of life, sometimes the direct route to an end is not the best solution. God works His will in ways that are sometimes mysterious to us. We must remember that He is operating on a much grander level than we can fathom. His will is weaving together events transcending time and space to accomplish His master plan.

> **"For My thoughts are not your thoughts, nor are your ways My ways," says the Lord. "For as the heavens are higher than the earth, so are My ways higher than your ways, and My thoughts than your thoughts."**
>
> —ISAIAH 55:8–9

God's ways will not always be the way we would choose to accomplish a task. We will not always understand, but when we are in reverent relationship with our Father, we can submit to His way and understand that He knows best.

> **On earth as it is in heaven.**
>
> —LUKE 11:2E

Yielding to God is not an event, but a lifestyle. Like any relationship, it takes work and commitment. Above all, it takes trust. When we are fully submitted to God, His way permeates our life. His will is baked into our every action, our walk.

> For we are His workmanship, created in Christ Jesus for good works, which God prepared beforehand that we should walk in them.
>
> —EPHESIANS 2:10

What does it mean for you to be God's workmanship created for good works?

We are created in God's own image, but we are human and flawed. Left to ourselves, we are incapable of good. Our good works are the direct result of our relationship with Christ Jesus through the Holy Spirit. Paul had a great deal of instruction for us regarding these good works, otherwise known as our "walk." By taking a few steps further in Ephesians, we will discover how to walk.

> I, therefore, the prisoner of the Lord, beseech you to walk worthy of the calling with which you were called, with all lowliness and gentleness, with longsuffering, bearing with one another in love, endeavoring to keep the unity of the Spirit in the bond of peace. There is one body and one Spirit, just as you were called in one hope of your calling; one Lord, one faith, one baptism; one God and Father of all, who is above all, and through all, and in you all.
>
> —EPHESIANS 4:1–6

Underline each word or phrase in the Ephesians passage that describes walking God's way.

Walking is action. So, let's act.

List each underlined word/phrase below. Then beside each word or phrase, write how you can act on that "way of God" in your daily walk.

As we continue to walk in God's ways, our relationship deepens and we become more and more like Him. We have a great example of what God is like in His Son, Jesus Christ. He is the flawless example of submission to God's way.

> Therefore be imitators of God as dear children. And walk in love, as Christ also has loved us and given Himself for us, an offering and a sacrifice to God for a sweet-smelling aroma.

> —EPHESIANS 5:1–2

I have often heard that imitation is the greatest form of flattery. We tend to imitate those we admire. Girls imitate their moms as they care for their dolls. Boys imitate superheroes as they save the day. How much more should we sincerely imitate Christ? This was encouraged several years ago with WWJD bracelets: What Would Jesus Do?

What opportunities do you have to imitate Christ in your daily walk?

As we begin to imitate Christ, it becomes a sweet-smelling aroma to our Father in heaven. This is a lifestyle of choosing God's way daily.

For you were once darkness, but now you are light in the Lord. Walk as children of light (for the fruit of the Spirit is in all goodness, righteousness, and truth), finding out what is acceptable to the Lord. And have no fellowship with the unfruitful works of darkness, but rather expose them. For it is shameful even to speak of those things which are done by them in secret.

—EPHESIANS 5:8–12

As children of light, we are to reflect Christ in every area of our lives. A mirror reflects the image of the one standing before it. We must keep Christ front and center in our lives so that we always reflect His light rather than the world's darkness.

Before we close today, let's look at one last direction from Paul regarding our daily walk.

See then that you walk circumspectly, not as fools but as wise, redeeming the time, because the days are evil. Therefore do not be unwise, but understand what the will of the Lord is. And do not be drunk with wine, in which is dissipation; but be filled with the Spirit, speaking to one another in psalms and hymns and spiritual songs, singing and making melody in your heart to the Lord, giving thanks always for all things to God the Father in the name of our Lord Jesus Christ, submitting to one another in the fear of God.

—EPHESIANS 5:15–21

As we glean wisdom from Paul's statement, what actions (or ways) are we to take in our daily walk?

What actions (or ways) are we to avoid?

Why does he end with submitting to one another? How does that connect with what we have learned so far?

We are to live intentionally with passion—controlled not by emotion but by passion for God's Word, His will, His ways, and His people. This passion only comes from close relationship with our Father.

I know this is a lot to absorb. God's will and ways are sometimes beyond our human understanding. We may never understand some of them this side of heaven. But of this we can be sure—God's way is the right way.

We will never understand everything in the Bible. If we follow what we do understand, we will do well. First and foremost, we should walk in love as Christ loved us, which is sacrificially. When we seek God's wisdom and direction, we will walk in the light.

Blessings!

> PRAYER: Show me Your ways, O Lord; Teach me Your paths.Lead me in Your truth and teach me, For You are the God of my salvation; On You I wait all the day.
> —PSALM 25:4–5

LESSON 8

Your Will, Your Way, Your Timing

I am not an avid football fan, but since my grandson decided to play, I am learning rules of the game. The passing game has always amazed me. Maybe because the calculation of where to throw the ball based on the speed of the receiver is somewhat mathematical. Timing is everything. If the timing is off, the pass will not be completed.

We have taken a slow and calculated look at the first verse of the Lord's Prayer. As we take a last look at what it means to request God's will, I would like to consider an element of submission that is not specifically mentioned, but I believe is fully implied. When we considered yielding to God's way, it was in respect to method. The "how" is extremely important. Today we will look at yielding to God's way with respect to timing. We can do what God asks of us by staying true to His method, but if our timing is not His timing, we will not be in God's perfect will.

Your will be done on earth as it is in heaven.

—LUKE 11:2D–2E

God created time as we understand it. In the first chapter of Genesis, we have record that God created light and separated it from darkness. He spun the earth just so, and the evening and morning became the first twenty-four-hour day. God caused the earth to rotate around the sun giving us seasons and our year. God stopped time in Joshua 10 to allow the children of Israel to have their revenge on their enemies. In Isaiah 38, God turned back time by ten degrees on the sundial as a sign to Hezekiah that He would extend the king's life by fifteen years. God is truly the Creator and Ruler of time.

One of the most well known passages regarding time comes from the wisdom God gave Solomon.

> To everything there is a season, a time for every purpose under heaven.

> —ECCLESIASTES 3:1

Solomon helps us understand that the timing of our purpose, to do God's will, is important. He goes on to give an extensive list of opposites and stating that each has its appropriate time. Today we will look at some key moments in Abraham's life to understand the importance of God's timing in our lives.

Please read Genesis 15:1–6. What did God promise Abram?

God went on to cut covenant with Abram, outlining the inheritance that would belong to his numerous descendants (see Genesis 15). After this historic revelation, we fast-forward ten years. Abram and Sarai remained childless.

Please read Genesis 16:1–4. Was this God's timing?

Continue reading Genesis 16:5–12. What were the consequences of Sarai and Abram's indiscretion?

Are you being tempted to run ahead of God today?

How does seeing these consequences encourage you to wait on God's timing in your situation?

Abram was eighty-six years old when Hagar the handmaid gave birth to the "wild man" Ishmael. He would wait thirteen more years before seeing God's timing come to pass. With the announcement of the coming birth, Abram and Sarai both received new names. Abram became Abraham, the father of many nations. Sarai became Sarah, the mother of nations. Let's look now at the conversation between God and Abraham.

Please read Genesis 17:17–22. What about this event assures you that it was God's timing?

The birth of Isaac is a great example of waiting on God's timing to be in His will. But what about the opposite? Are there times when we need to act immediately to stay in God's will? Let's fast-forward a few years in Isaacs's life and see an example of this very thing.

Please read Genesis 22:1–19. Describe how God chose to test Abraham's faith.

Abraham's response to God's direction is noteworthy. Abraham's relationship with God surely grew in the years after Isaac's birth. He did not try to change God's direction. He did not try to avoid the task. He started early and did what God commanded without delay. He followed God's direction to the letter. There is no record of bargaining or begging for a different path. He simply obeyed God's direction until he received further direction.

When Isaac questioned what would happen, Abraham's response was solid. God will provide. And God did. The angel's call to Abraham was urgent. Abraham was taking care of business and the angel had to act quickly to intervene. Abraham, Isaac, and all their descendants were blessed by Abraham's acts of obedience.

In the first instance, Abram had to wait for God's timing of the promised child. In the second, Abraham was rewarded for instant response. How do we know when to wait and when to act? The answer is in the Word of God! Look again at God's words to Abram regarding a child.

> And behold, the word of the Lord came to him, saying, "This one shall not be your heir, but one who will come from your own body shall be your heir." Then He brought him outside and said, "Look now toward heaven, and count the stars if you are able to number them." And He said to him, "So shall your descendants be."
>
> —GENESIS 15:4–5

Does God tell Abram to do anything?

Look again at God's direction to Abraham regarding the sacrifice of Isaac.

> Then He said, "Take now your son, your only son Isaac, whom you love, and go to the land of Moriah, and offer him there as a burnt offering on one of the mountains of which I shall tell you."

> —GENESIS 22:2

Does God tell Abraham to do anything?

And there it is. To do God's will in His timing we must first listen fully to God's direction. God promised Abram he would have descendants, but He never told him to do anything to make it happen. It was a promise that God would fulfill in His own timing. Later God told Abraham not only to take Isaac and sacrifice him, but to do it now. God gave specific direction for Abraham to follow.

What direction are you receiving from God today? Are you following?

As we build a relationship with our heavenly Father, our ears will become more intent on hearing His direction. Sometimes He offers the soothing promise that His will is going to happen. Sometimes He gives us directions to follow to accomplish His will. An intimate relationship with our Father is required to clearly hear the difference.

Blessings!

> **PRAYER:** Thank God for the promises He has given you in His Word. Ask Him for direction to stay in His perfect will, way, and timing. Then listen.

SECTION 3:

LIVING WITH PROVISION

No matter our age, provision is a huge part of our lives. Some provision is earthly. When we were babies, our caretakers provided food, clothing, and shelter for us. We were helpless without that provision. As we grew, we were given more and more responsibility to begin providing for ourselves. A clean room. A made bed. Later, spending money from chores, then a part time job, and ultimately full time employment.

As adults, we tend to think we provide for ourselves, but it is not possible without heavenly provision. "Every good gift and every perfect gift" is from our Father in heaven (James 1:17). God never wavers in His provision. If we think He has wavered, we probably don't understand His plan.

God's provision is not conditional. He provided clothing for Adam and Eve in the form of animal skins. Even though they had disobeyed Him, He provided for their needs. As Abraham acted in obedience, God provided a ram for sacrifice in place of Isaac. He later provided safe passage for Abraham's descendants, those stiff-necked Israelites, to the land He had promised them many years before.

The most important provision came in the form of a Baby. God provided salvation by sending His one and only Son as a sacrifice for our sins. In addition to salvation, He provides the Holy Spirit to live within us, guide us, and direct us. Then He provides an eternal heavenly home for us, His children. God's provision is steady and faithful.

We now stand at a pivotal point in the model prayer. Until now the prayer has been focused on God—who He is, who we are in Him, and our relationship with Him. Only after we understand this relationship can we make appropriate requests. This is the point where the gospels of Matthew and Luke begin to differ slightly in the passages on Jesus's model prayer. We will explore both versions as we have much to learn from each one.

In this section, we will discover the breadth and depth of the provision that is possible from our heavenly Father. When we ask appropriately, our loving Father will provide. Let's learn together how to live abundantly within God's perfect provision.

Blessings!

LESSON 9

Give Us

"Give me! Give me! Give me!" is a predictable rant of a strong-willed child intent on receiving what *they* desire. It's part of our sin nature to value what *we* want above what others want and, at times, even above what is best for us. This is why we should begin our conversations with God by acknowledging Him as Lord and King. It puts us in the right mindset to ask Him for the right things.

> **Give us day by day our daily bread.**
>
> —LUKE 11:3

Matthew's record of the model prayer given during the Sermon on the Mount phrases is slightly different. This is the wording that is burned in my memory.

> **Give us this day our daily bread.**
>
> —MATTHEW 6:11

This one request is packed with so much information. We will spend this entire section unpacking it and understanding exactly what this request tells us about a relationship with our heavenly Father.

Our requests begin with two simple words, "give us." As we have studied before, all mention of God is in singular form, but all mention of His children is plural. This is a subtle reminder that this is not a "give me" request, but a request to "give us," your children. Paul expanded on this in his first letter to Timothy.

> First of all, then, I urge that petitions, prayers, intercessions, and thanksgivings be made for everyone, for kings and all those who are in authority, so that we may lead a tranquil and quiet life in all godliness and dignity. This is good, and it pleases God our Savior, who wants everyone to be saved and to come to the knowledge of the truth.

> —1 TIMOTHY 2:1–4 (HCSB)

There are three basic components to this passage. Paul lists the categories of prayer and for whom we are to pray. Then he lists the results of a God-pleasing prayer. Let's begin with the categories and weave in the other components as we go.

Please list the four categories of prayer mentioned in this passage.

Now let's dive into those one by one. First, we have petitions or specific requests. Since we are praying for our heavenly Father to "give us," these petitions will be for our specific needs and the needs of others. We are to make requests on behalf of our leaders. Praying for our leaders is paired with tranquil and quiet lives. When our leaders are bathed in prayer, our quality of life will be improved. Verse 4 gives us a very important request that the unsaved will come to a knowledge of the truth and be saved. Paul gives the Philippians further information about these requests.

> Be anxious for nothing, but in everything by prayer and supplication, with thanksgiving, let your requests be made known to God; and the peace of God, which surpasses all understanding, will guard your hearts and minds through Christ Jesus.

> —PHILIPPIANS 4:6–7

We are not to be anxious or worried about the things we lay at the Father's feet. Anxiousness and God's peace cannot coexist. We are not promised that God will always grant our requests, but must continue to pray under the umbrella of God's will. We are promised that He will guard our hearts with His peace, surpassing all human understanding, in the matter. If our request is not within His will, then He will give us peace in the outcome that is His will.

What are some petitions (specific requests) you are currently bringing to God?

Now expand on these petitions in a way that emphasizes God as our Provider.

The next category of prayer is simply labeled "prayer." Wiersbe explains this form of prayer.

> Prayers is the commonest term for this activity, and it emphasizes the sacredness of prayer. We are praying to God; prayer is an act of worship, not just an expression of our wants and needs. There should be reverence in our hearts as we pray to God.[1]
>
> —WARREN WIERSBE

Does that sound vaguely familiar? If so, you have been paying attention! Wiersbe connects prayer back to the reverence and submission Jesus taught in the first part of the model prayer. Prayer is communication, but it is also very much an act of worship. Our heavenly Father is worthy to be praised.

Our third category of prayer is intercession. At first glance, this appears similar to requests. But look closely. Almost every mention of intercession in the New Testament refers to Jesus and the Holy Spirit interceding for us. If intercession is something practiced within the Trinity, how are we to emulate intercession? We look to Christ for His example. As He walked this earth in human form, He was the perfect example of how we should live. That includes intercession. In His last hours on the cross, He gave us a perfect example of intercession.

> There were also two others, criminals, led with Him to be put to death. And when they had come to the place called Calvary, there they crucified Him, and the criminals, one on the right hand and the other on the left. Then Jesus said, "Father, forgive them, for they do not know what they do." And they divided His garments and cast lots.
>
> —LUKE 23:32–34

Even while hanging on the cross in excruciating pain, Jesus interceded for the men who put Him there. We know Jesus's crucifixion was God's will because in the garden Jesus prayed that if it were not, God would let it pass from Him. It was God's plan for salvation. It had to happen. Then Jesus compassionately asked the Father to forgive His persecutors.

Sometimes bad things happen to seemingly good people. Unlike Jesus, we may never know why some things happen to us. We are not often privy to God's master plan. However, if we have faith and do our best to live in God's will, we can be sure there is a reason greater than our knowledge. If we can keep the faith that God has a plan for us and He is working out that plan in our lives, then we can have peace that allows us to intercede for those who have wronged us. This peace is a sweet, tender, and intimate place in our relationship with the Savior.

Who has wronged you today?

Are you at a point in your relationship with the Father that you can intercede for them? Write that prayer here.

Not there yet? I understand, as does our Savior. He knows our hearts. If our requests are open and honest, He will guide us to that place of peace where we can pray for our persecutors.

Finally, we arrive at the prayer of thanksgiving. God is so good! If He provided nothing other than salvation, that would be so much more than we deserve. We will never be able to praise and thank Him enough. That is only the beginning of His provision for us. We will explore that concept tomorrow!

Until then, blessings!

PRAYER: Thank God for your salvation. Thank Him for His bountiful provision in your life. Be specific when you thank Him for His blessings.

LESSON 10

Give Us Bread

My family tries to have a family night each week, which includes a family meal. We normally order from a local restaurant and have the meal delivered. Each week the question is asked, what are we going to eat tonight? It's normally answered quickly, food is ordered, and the night goes on. Without a specific answer, we cannot share a family meal. Without specific details, we may be surprised by what ends up on, or is missing from, our plates.

> **Give us this day our daily bread.**
>
> —MATTHEW 6:11

Bread. On the surface, it's such a basic provision. After all, a person can survive on bread and water. But our Father doesn't desire for us to simply survive. He wants us to thrive. Bread has a much richer meaning.

While this request for bread may seem simplistic at the surface, it is quite specific. The amount is specific. The provision is specific. Even the timing is specific. When it comes to requesting provision, our Father desires specificity. Getting specific with our requests requires that we be open and honest about our insufficiencies. The more intimate our relationship with the Father, the more specific we become with Him.

Which of your requests today need to be more specific?

Express to your Father your exact need.

Jesus's instruction to ask for bread also gives us direction in what to request. Bread was a staple food in Jesus's day, as it is today. A staple food is eaten routinely and is a basic part of a standard diet. It's not expected to be extravagant or expensive, just steady and necessary. This speaks volumes about the type of provision we should seek.

> **And my God shall supply all your need according to His riches in glory by Christ Jesus.**
>
> —PHILIPPIANS 4:19

This is not to say our Father is cheap or skimps on our provision. Quite the opposite. He owns the cattle of a thousand hills. He provides for our needs out of His riches in glory. But it is only our needs that He promises, not our wants. Sometimes He does bless us with our wants, but it's not promised.

So how do we know what to ask? What is the specific "bread" we need today? The first clue is found in the prayer we are studying. "Your will be done." Every provision should be requested within God's will. If we are unsure if our request is in God's will, we can follow Jesus's example and start with "If it's Your will, Father."

What are you requesting that you are unsure is in God's will? Write that prayer now, preceding it with "If it's Your will, Father. . ."

Another way to know if our request is acceptable is to precede it with another request. Ask God for wisdom in the matter.

> **If any of you lacks wisdom, let him ask of God, who gives to all liberally and without reproach, and it will be given to him.**
>
> —JAMES 1:5

Ask our Father for wisdom and then listen. Be still in your quiet place and allow His wisdom to wash over you.

Remember that God is not on our timetable. His wisdom may not come immediately. He may provide wisdom through His Word, which requires study. He may provide wisdom through a pastor or Sunday School teacher, which requires attendance and attention. His wisdom may become evident through a song, which requires worship. He speaks to us through many avenues. Our goal should be to always listen for His whisper of truth.

In what area are you currently seeking God's wisdom?

In what avenues are you listening?

Bread not only represents physical provision but also represents spiritual provision. Spiritual hunger is a requirement for spiritual growth and relationship building.

> **And Jesus said to them, "I am the bread of life. He who comes to Me shall never hunger, and he who believes in Me shall never thirst."**
>
> —JOHN 6:35

Spiritual hunger is a God-given hunger that grows stronger the more we feed it. The more we experience the Bread of Life, the more we will want to experience Him. Our request for bread should always include our request for spiritual nourishment. We should always be found wanting more. Our cravings should be for a deeper relationship with our Father through Jesus Christ, the Bread of Life.

While this lesson is about specificity, I also realize there are times when we simply don't know the specifics. We are without words. Our feelings overflow but our words will not form. For times like this, sweet friend, provision has already been made.

> **In the same way, the Spirit helps us in our weakness. We do not know what we ought to pray for, but the Spirit himself intercedes for us through wordless groans. And he who searches our hearts knows the mind of the Spirit, because the Spirit intercedes for God's people in accordance with the will of God.**
>
> —ROMANS 8:26–27 (NIV)

In times of deepest pain, when we feel like we cannot utter a word, the Holy Spirit within us takes over. Through our groans, He speaks to the Father on our behalf. Is that not the sweetest promise? I have heard God's love described as a blanket. I feel that blanket of love wrapped around me when I read this promise. When all I can do is cry, the Spirit intercedes for me. He requests God's will for my situation. This is when we are firmly under the shadow of His mighty wings. We are protected and secure. We are loved beyond measure. We are feasting on heavenly bread.

Where are you today? Do you firmly understand your specific need that is within God's will? Keep asking and He will provide in His perfect time. Do you feel the need but are unsure of the "God's will" provision you should be asking for? Keep seeking His wisdom. Study. Attend. Worship. He will show you the answer in His time.

Is this the day you are at the end of your rope? You have no words left to say? Tie a knot in that rope, dear sister, and hang on. The Holy Spirit will come to your rescue. I cannot promise He will pull you right up from that pit. Oh, how I wish I could promise that. But I can promise He has a plan that will ultimately bring glory to Him. Trust Him. He will wrap His blanket of love around you and tuck you right under His mighty wing until the storm passes by. And it will pass, in His time.

I hope it encourages you to know the Father wants this level of intimate conversation with you. He knows our needs before we ask. He wants us to understand He is the great Provider.

Blessings!

PRAYER: Whatever your current situation , our Father is there also. Talk to Him. Express your need and your confidence that He will provide in His perfect time.

LESSON 11

Give Us Today

We can know a product or service has achieved success when its brand becomes the representation of the product or service. Here are a few examples. We ask for a Kleenex when we want a tissue. When we hear La-Z-Boy, we immediately think recliner. We Google things rather than search. If we are offered a Coke in the southern United States, it really means, do we want a soda? These brands have become interchangeable with the name of the product.

All retailers have felt the pain of the Amazon Effect. When one-day and same-day delivery became possible, it became expected of everyone. Sadly, we sometimes apply the Amazon Effect to God. We expect one day or even same day delivery on all our requests. Thankfully, God operates on a different, much higher, level than Amazon.

Give us this day our daily bread.

—MATTHEW 6:11

As we continue to look at specificity, note that "this day" is very specific. We are eager to ask for delivery today. What we fail to recognize is that delivery is for today's need. Not tomorrow or the next day. Just today. What do I really need today?

Write today's date in the space below.

Now use the chart below to list the provisions you are currently asking from the Father. Divide them into what you must have today and what can wait until a later date.

Today's needs:	Future needs:

Was today's list shorter than you expected? There are times when we are in absolute dire need of provision. Most of the time, we just need provision soon. Jesus narrows our focus to "this day." What do I truly need today? We find that answer in Matthew 6:

> Therefore I say to you, do not worry about your life, what you will eat or what you will drink; nor about your body, what you will put on. Is not life more than food and the body more than clothing? Look at the birds of the air, for they neither sow nor reap nor gather into barns; yet your heavenly Father feeds them. Are you not of more value than they? Which of you by worrying can add one cubit to his stature?
>
> So why do you worry about clothing? Consider the lilies of the field, how they grow: they neither toil nor spin; and yet I say to you that even Solomon in all his glory was not arrayed like one of these. Now if God so clothes the grass of the field, which today is, and tomorrow is thrown into the oven, will He not much more clothe you, O you of little faith?

Therefore do not worry, saying, "What shall we eat?" or "What shall we drink?" or "What shall we wear?" For after all these things the Gentiles seek. For your heavenly Father knows that you need all these things. But seek first the kingdom of God and His righteousness, and all these things shall be added to you. Therefore do not worry about tomorrow, for tomorrow will worry about its own things. Sufficient for the day is its own trouble.

— MATTHEW 6:25–34

According to Jesus, our first need for this day is the kingdom of God and His righteousness. When our focus is on Him, He will take care of our physical needs. We may not have all our wants, but we will have what we need to fulfill His will today.

Five hundred years ago, Michel de Montaigne said, "My life has been filled with terrible misfortune; most of which never happened."[1] We worry about so many things. A health article about the effects of worry on the brain reported the findings of one study:

It turns out that 85 percent of what subjects worried about never happened, and with the 15 percent that did happen, 79 percent of subjects discovered either they could handle the difficulty better than expected, or the difficulty taught them a lesson worth learning. This means that 97 percent of what you worry over is not much more than a fearful mind punishing you with exaggerations and misperceptions.[2]

Let's do the math:

o   85% of worries never happened.
o   12% experienced their worry.
    o   They handled it better than they expected.
    o   It taught them something.
o   3% experienced their worry with no benefit.

I dare say, there was something for the 3% to learn and they missed it. Our challenge today is to skip the worry and lean into our faith. We want to see what God wants to teach us, no matter what does or does not happen. Let's see if we can prove this point.

Name something you worried about that never happened.

Name something that happened and you were able to handle better than you expected.

Name something that happened and God taught you something through it.

I am writing this lesson during the 2020 Covid-19 pandemic. We have experienced sheltering in place, furloughs, and closures. We can't see people smile because everyone is wearing a mask. It's very true that sufficient for the day is its own trouble!

Even in a pandemic, God knows what we need before we ask. The call to focus on today is the call to faith that God holds tomorrow. Nothing ever surprises God. Everything that happens in our lives is either orchestrated by Him or allowed by Him. And every time it is for a purpose: His purpose and His plan and His glory.

> **"For I know the plans I have for you," says the Lord. "They are plans for good and not for disaster, to give you a future and a hope."**
>
> —JEREMIAH 29:11 (NLT)

When we focus on His presence and His plan today, He *will* prosper us. We all know that to prosper doesn't always mean to be wealthy. The greatest prospering is spiritual. After all, what we can see is temporary but what we cannot see is eternal.

Blessings!

PRAYER: What is your greatest need today? Petition the Father for today's provision.

LESSON 12

Give Us Daily

Let's imagine for a moment that you are going to the family doctor for an ailment of some sort. The doctor examines you and prescribes one pill per day for ten days. Easy enough, right? You take the prescription to a pharmacy and then take a little bottle home. Do you empty the bottle and count the pills? Or do you trust there are enough pills in the bottle for each day prescribed? If you trust the pharmacist, you are not surprised to find enough pills for each day.

> **Give us day by day our daily bread.**
>
> —LUKE 11:3

This week we are exploring God's provision for us. The great Physician is directing us to come to Him with our need for the day. Each day we are to request our supply for that day. If we trust our family doctor and pharmacist to provide what we need, how much more trust should we place in our heavenly Father the great Physician?

When you think of the first person you trusted, who comes to mind? Why?

While I recognize that some people had a difficult childhood, many of us place our earliest feelings of trust with a family member. Whether it was a strong father figure, a hard-working mother figure, or a larger than life older sibling, family ties generally are threaded with some level of trust and security.

> **If a son asks for bread from any father among you, will he give him a stone? Or if he asks for a fish, will he give him a serpent instead of a fish? Or if he asks for an egg, will he offer him a scorpion? If you then, being evil, know how to give good gifts to your children, how much more will your heavenly Father give the Holy Spirit to those who ask Him!**
>
> —LUKE 11:11–13

Jesus gave this example of provision immediately following the model prayer. He expanded the idea by giving an example all would understand, the love of a father. Then He asked the rhetorical question, how much more will your heavenly Father give? I find it extremely interesting that the Father's gift is not material but spiritual. Our heavenly Father gives us the Holy Spirit abundantly when we ask Him. Through the Holy Spirit we are provided guidance and wisdom from above, which we can daily trust and depend on.

The greatest example of daily physical provision can be found in Exodus. Let's examine the faithful provision of Father God as we join Moses and the Israelites in the wilderness.

> **Then the Lord said to Moses, "Behold, I will rain bread from heaven for you. And the people shall go out and gather a certain quota every day, that I may test them, whether they will walk in My law or not. And it shall be on the sixth day that they shall prepare what they bring in, and it shall be twice as much as they gather daily."**
>
> —EXODUS 16:4–5

Please underline "every day."

For forty years, God provided manna from heaven to nourish the children of Israel. Their clothes and shoes never wore out. God provided their need for each day and asked them to trust Him. He directed them to gather a quota of manna every day. He did not direct them to hoard up resources. He directed them to take only what they needed for the day and trust that provision would be there every day. In the same way, Jesus directed us to focus on what we need today, while acknowledging and trusting in His day-by-day provision.

Please underline "test them."

In Exodus, God was testing the Israelites. Would they trust Him to provide for them day-by-day? They had trusted the Egyptians to provide food. According to the Israelites, they had sat around pots of food and eaten until they were full (Exodus 16:3). God had just parted the Red Sea and provided their way of escape and yet they did not trust Him to provide for other needs. They trusted the Egyptians who enslaved them, but not the God who freed them.

> So when the children of Israel saw it, they said to one another, "What is it?" For they did not know what it was.
>
> And Moses said to them, "This is the bread which the Lord has given you to eat. This is the thing which the Lord has commanded: 'Let every man gather it according to each one's need, one omer for each person, according to the number of persons; let every man take for those who are in his tent.'"
>
> Then the children of Israel did so and gathered, some more, some less. So when they measured it by omers, he who gathered much had nothing left over, and he who gathered little had no lack. Every man had gathered according to each one's need. And Moses said, "Let no one leave any of it till morning." Notwithstanding they did not heed Moses. But some of them left part of it until morning, and it bred worms and stank. And Moses was angry with them.

> So they gathered it every morning, every man according to his
> need. And when the sun became hot, it melted.
>
> —EXODUS 16:15–21

We can easily shake our heads at these Israelites and wonder why they didn't trust God, but do we sometimes suffer from the same lack of confidence in God? Do we trust our employer, our bank account, or the stock market more than the God who saved us?

Who do you trust today for your provision?

What provision are you trying to hoard today? What action can you take to show that you trust God to provide daily?

Even though the children of Israel didn't always trust God as they should, He continued to faithfully provide for them. This is a beautiful picture of God's daily faithfulness to provide for His people.

> And the children of Israel ate manna forty years, until they came
> to an inhabited land; they ate manna until they came to the border
> of the land of Canaan.
>
> —EXODUS 16:35

God wanted them to trust that He would provide. And He did provide manna for them to eat until He delivered them into the land of Canaan where He continued to provide in a different way. He wants the same from us today. He wants us to trust Him to provide what we need this day and every day forward.

In the middle of whatever is going on in my life and yours, we can trust that God is providing daily what we need to honor and glorify Him. Sister, that's all we need.

Blessings!

PRAYER: Ask the Lord to forgive you for times when you did not trust Him and to help your faith to grow stronger as you witness daily His loving provision for you.

SECTION 4:

LIVING FORGIVEN

Forgiveness is a funny thing. We frequently desire forgiveness (from God, from friends, from family) but we seldom rush to extend the same. I know people who hold on to perceived wrongs committed against them decades ago. They let them simmer in their hearts and pollute their minds.

> **To be a Christian means to forgive the inexcusable because God has forgiven the inexcusable in you.**[1]
>
> ——C. S. LEWIS

When it comes to forgiveness, God never wants us to drag our feet and let unforgiveness fester. He wants us to follow His divine example and go above and beyond what is required.

> **Then Peter came to Him and said, "Lord, how often shall my brother sin against me, and I forgive him? Up to seven times?"**
>
> **Jesus said to him, "I do not say to you, up to seven times, but up to seventy times seven."**
>
> —MATTHEW 18:21–22

Jesus wasn't implying we should keep account of wrongs against us up to a limit that was a point of no return. On the contrary, His seventy times seven was an exaggeration that implied no limits.

In what is commonly known as the "Love Chapter," Paul describes the characteristics of love in the life of a Christian. Among these, we find that love keeps no record of wrongs (1 Corinthians 13:5 HCSB). Even if we tried to keep a record and did not lose count, we would hopefully develop a practice of forgiving well before reaching 490. Whether we lose interest in counting or find that forgiveness is the best practice, we will never reach Jesus's level of forgiveness.

The model prayer has a lot to say on forgiveness. In this section, we will explore what it means to truly live both forgiven and forgiving.

Blessings!

LESSON 13

Forgiven Sins

What comes to mind when you think about a rebel? No one enjoys a rebellious child who acts up and defies authority. But when an adult is called a rebel, it carries a different meaning. A rebel is spontaneous, a risk taker, someone who marches to the beat of their own drum. Movies have glorified the concept. The truth is that rebellion brings no glory to God. In fact, rebellion against God is outright sin. It causes us to miss His purpose for our lives. When we rebel, we submit to worldly temptations rather than to the will of our heavenly Father. Is there really glory in being a rebel?

> **And forgive us our sins, for we also forgive everyone who is indebted to us.**
>
> —LUKE 11:4A

In today's section of the model prayer, we are being very transparent. First, we admit our rebellion and sin, because we all fall short. Sin is a daily occurrence and forgiveness is a daily need. We are to ask forgiveness humbly, knowing that Jesus paid the price for our sins. If we deny our sin, then we deny the need for our Savior. Our relationship with God depends on this transparent and humble request for forgiveness. Take a moment to be real with yourself.

Record your unconfessed sin, whether mentally or in writing. Ask God for forgiveness right now.

Doesn't that feel good? A clean slate! Forgiven. Unfortunately, it doesn't take us long as sinful humans to mess that slate up again. This is a daily practice. Confess and seek forgiveness. The deeper our relationship with Him, the more we understand that His mercies are new every morning. Great is His faithfulness to forgive (see Lamentations 3:22–23).

It would be so easy to stop right there. We are forgiven! Yay! Now let's move on. But Jesus didn't stop there, and neither should we. We can ask God to forgive us for we are also willing to forgive. Forgive whom? Everyone who is indebted to us. Well, that is asking a lot. I mean, you know that woman who did that thing to me. She doesn't deserve forgiveness ... but wait. Did I deserve the forgiveness I just asked of our Father?

Notice that we are to forgive everyone who is indebted to us. We are forgiving indebtedness, not sin. Only God has the authority to deal with sin. That is above our pay grade. Our job is to see their debt to us and forgive that, which is confusing to me. What does that look like? Let's back up to the Sermon on the Mount and see how Jesus explains this concept.

> But I say to you who hear: Love your enemies, do good to those who hate you, bless those who curse you, and pray for those who spitefully use you. To him who strikes you on the one cheek, offer the other also. And from him who takes away your cloak, do not withhold your tunic either. Give to everyone who asks of you. And from him who takes away your goods do not ask them back. And just as you want men to do to you, you also do to them likewise.

> —LUKE 6:27–31

Jesus is asking us to respond to others with love rather than react with judgment. Does someone hate you? Pray for them. Has someone landed a blow to your cheek, physically or figuratively? Don't swing back. Take the high road and turn the other cheek. Has someone taken something from you? Don't fight to get it back. See their need through Jesus's eyes and meet their need in an even larger way. Be generous and live with open hands, not clenched fists. Revenge is a bitter dish, but love goes down sweetly.

Does anyone in your life fall into one or more of these categories? How will you respond with love?

It sure isn't easy, but it is Christlike. Let God take care of dealing with sin. That's His specialty. We are to be so thankful for our undeserved forgiveness that we spread love, kindness, and forgiveness freely and abundantly throughout our lives to everyone. Especially those indebted to us.

Blessings!

> PRAYER: Ask God to show you today where you need to spread some forgiveness and love. Then go!

LESSON 14

Forgiven Debts

"I owe, I owe, so off to work I go!" can regularly be seen on bumper stickers across California and I daresay many other states. Somehow, I don't think they are singing to the same happy tune as Snow White's dwarves. Debt is a nasty four-letter word. Many have spent their lives battling it while others have made their living teaching us how to avoid it. In Matthew's account of the model prayer in the Sermon on the Mount, Jesus changed the wording slightly. While in Luke He instructed us to ask forgiveness for our sins, here He directed us to ask forgiveness of our debts. This wording is no less or more than the wording in Luke. Both are the Word of God and should be equally explored for our edification.

> **And forgive us our debts, as we forgive our debtors.**
>
> —MATTHEW 6:12

What is the difference between asking God to forgive sin and asking Him to forgive debt?

The word "debt" indicates a payment that is owed. Our sins amass a huge amount of debt. What is that debt? Paul tells us in his letter to the Roman church that the wages of sin is death (see Romans 6:23).

As with any other debt, it does require payment. Throughout the Old Testament, we see the Israelites sacrifice sin offerings as a means of payment. Their sacrifice was flawed, therefore only an installment and never enough to completely settle the debt. Their sacrifices continued over and over.

> But if we walk in the light as He is in the light, we have fellowship with one another, and the blood of Jesus Christ His Son cleanses us from all sin. If we say that we have no sin, we deceive ourselves, and the truth is not in us. If we confess our sins, He is faithful and just to forgive us our sins and to cleanse us from all unrighteousness.
>
> —1 JOHN 1:7–9

When we ask God to forgive our sins, we acknowledge that we understand our need for forgiveness. When we ask God to forgive our debts, we acknowledge that we understand the cost of forgiveness.

Jesus was the spotless perfect sacrifice. He paid the debt we could never pay. We can humbly ask our Father to forgive our sin debt only because Jesus has already paid the price.

Jesus's blood cleanses us from all sin. Not just yesterday's sin. Not just this week's sin. All sin—past, present, and future. No further sacrifice is recorded in Scripture because no further sacrifice is needed. Jesus paid it all. Paid in full. We are forgiven.

How does it make you feel to know your debt has been paid?

And forgive us our debts, as we forgive our debtors.

—MATTHEW 6:12

Just as in Luke's account, there is a comma and not a period. The meaning of debt does not change. Debt means something is owed. And forgiveness of that debt means that the debtor doesn't pay. Who are our debtors? Let's pick up where we left off in the last lesson and see what Jesus has to say.

> **But if you love those who love you, what credit is that to you? For even sinners love those who love them. And if you do good to those who do good to you, what credit is that to you? For even sinners do the same. And if you lend to those from whom you hope to receive back, what credit is that to you? For even sinners lend to sinners to receive as much back. But love your enemies, do good, and lend, hoping for nothing in return; and your reward will be great, and you will be sons of the Most High. For He is kind to the unthankful and evil. Therefore be merciful, just as your Father also is merciful.**

—LUKE 6:32–36

Our heavenly Father loved us so much that He extended mercy in the form of His Son. He gave His one and only Son as payment for our sin debt. When we were unthankful and evil, He showed us overwhelming mercy and love. That is what we are asked to do. Because He forgave our debt, we are to forgive our debtors with the same love and mercy.

We are to love the unlovable, be good to people even when they are not good to us, and be generous. Give freely and unconditionally. Lending expects payment. Forgive that debt and expect nothing. Forgiving frees our hearts and minds to focus on what is important and eternal.

What debt do you need to forgive today? How will you do that?

Forgive freely and enjoy God's forgiveness.

Blessings!

PRAYER: Ask our Father today to reveal to you those debts you continue to hold. Then forgive.

LESSON 15

Forgiven Brothers

I am blessed with two brothers and two sisters, who are all older than me. I have always looked up to and thought very highly of my siblings. I know some families are not as blessed, but our sibling relationships should be some of the strongest relationships we have. Blood is thicker than water, right? Through the blood of Christ, we are all siblings with Christ. We are children of God. There should be a sibling bond among Christians that is hard to sever.

So, what happens when that bond is damaged? How should we deal with our sisters and brothers in Christ? I'm glad you asked. Jesus addresses this in the Sermon on the Mount.

> You have heard that it was said to those of old, "You shall not murder, and whoever murders will be in danger of the judgment." But I say to you that whoever is angry with his brother without a cause shall be in danger of the judgment. And whoever says to his brother, "Raca!" shall be in danger of the council. But whoever says, "You fool!" shall be in danger of hell fire. Therefore if you bring your gift to the altar, and there remember that your brother has something against you, leave your gift there before the altar, and go your way. First be reconciled to your brother, and then come and offer your gift.
>
> —MATTHEW 5:21–24

I have heard it said that we must get our horizontal relationships right before we can expect our vertical relationship to be what it needs to be. When our earthly (horizontal) relationships with believers are severed, it can greatly impact our ability to communicate with the Father (vertical relationship). We must first reconcile with our brothers and sisters in Christ before offering gifts to God.

What "gifts" is this passage referring to in the context of our lives?

In Jesus's day, physical sacrifices were brought to the altar. Jesus instructed His listeners to put down their sacrifice, repair the relationship with their brother, and then come into the presence of God. The vertical relationship cannot be celebrated until the horizontal relationship has been repaired.

We learned in Lesson 6 that, this side of the cross, we are to be a living sacrifice fully submitted to the Father. Our lives, the use of our spiritual gifts, and the use of our talents are all to be holy and acceptable to God. We are to honor and glorify Him with our full being. However, if we have broken relationships with other Christians, how can we fully glorify Him? We must stop and fix the problem.

> **Judge not, that you be not judged. For with what judgment you judge, you will be judged; and with the measure you use, it will be measured back to you. And why do you look at the speck in your brother's eye, but do not consider the plank in your own eye? Or how can you say to your brother, "Let me remove the speck from your eye"; and look, a plank is in your own eye? Hypocrite! First remove the plank from your own eye, and then you will see clearly to remove the speck from your brother's eye.**
>
> —MATTHEW 7:1–5

God is the Judge of all. If we presume to have the right to judge, we would be trying to take God's position. We are so unworthy to do that. When we pass judgment on others, we are asking to be judged by the same measuring stick. I choose mercy every time. When we show mercy to our Christian siblings, then we can receive mercy instead of judgment when our own eye is inspected.

Our relationship with the Father is so much richer when we love, respect, and forgive His children.

What child of God needs your mercy today? How can you show them God's love and forgiveness?

I hope this lesson has made your heart tender for your siblings in Christ. Build up your relationships in Christ. Love your siblings. You will be blessed!

Blessings!

PRAYER: Ask the Father to soften your heart toward your siblings in Christ. Then show them love and forgiveness.

LESSON 16

Forgiven Others

We have discussed forgiving those who have sinned against us, those who owe us something, and our brothers and sisters. But what about the average Joe or Jane? What about those who have not harmed us, but through the curse of social media (or the rumor mill), we know their business and their faults? What about forgiving others?

It is so easy to pass judgment on people we don't really know. We see a picture here and hear a whisper there and suddenly, we are in fully robed judgment banging our gavel and casting a guilty verdict on an unsuspecting acquaintance.

Have you ever been judgmental toward someone for something you have done in your own past?

He who cannot forgive others destroys the bridge over which he himself must pass.[1]

—GEORGE HERBERT

Express in your own words what this quote means to you.

This quote brings me face to face with a very revealing mirror. I have made bad decisions. I have fallen short. I need forgiveness. How can I ask God and others for forgiveness when I am unwilling to extend the same love to others? Isn't that what forgiveness really is? To love like Christ.

The way we relate to others shows how much God's Word and His love have taken root in our hearts. If we don't feel God's love for others in our hearts and we burn the bridges of forgiveness so they cannot cross, then we have no bridge of love and forgiveness to cross ourselves. In Matthew 6, Jesus immediately followed the model prayer with this charge reinforcing the severity of an unforgiving spirit.

> For if you forgive men their trespasses, your heavenly Father will also forgive you. But if you do not forgive men their trespasses, neither will your Father forgive your trespasses.

—MATTHEW 6:14–15

After His triumphal entry into Jerusalem, Jesus again stressed the importance of forgiveness and how it affects a relationship with God.

> So Jesus answered and said to them, "Have faith in God. For assuredly, I say to you, whoever says to this mountain, 'Be removed and be cast into the sea,' and does not doubt in his heart, but believes that those things he says will be done, he will

have whatever he says. Therefore I say to you, whatever things you ask when you pray, believe that you receive them, and you will have them.

"And whenever you stand praying, if you have anything against anyone, forgive him, that your Father in heaven may also forgive you your trespasses. But if you do not forgive, neither will your Father in heaven forgive your trespasses."

—MARK 11:22–26

Jesus gives us a beautiful picture of faith immediately followed by a directive to forgive. Faith and forgiveness live hand in hand. One doesn't really exist without the other. We cannot communicate in full, unbroken relationships with our heavenly Father when we have unforgiveness in our hearts. We are to forgive immediately, not tomorrow or when we feel like it, or when our anger subsides. He simply directs us to forgive. Now. Then we can go about our conversation with the Father.

If anyone doubts the reach of our obligation to forgive, it is settled in verse 25. If we have anything against anyone, forgive him or her. That is specific and inclusive. Name one trespass that isn't covered by the word "anything." There are none. Then name one person not covered by the word "anyone." No one. It's everyone everywhere who has done anything, large or small, that you hold against them. Jesus said to forgive them. If we refuse, we walk in disobedience. Our fellowship with the Father is broken until we obey.

Are you withholding forgiveness from someone today? How will you transform this into forgiveness and mercy?

Please remember that we are not directed to *forgive* their sin. That is God's work. We are to forgive and love the sinner just as we desire to be forgiven and loved. They may not deserve forgiveness, but neither do we. We are all in the same boat when it comes to what we deserve. We are equally guilty. We are equally unworthy. We are equally lost. Yet we are equally forgiven by the shed blood of Jesus Christ. Amen!

> **And be kind to one another, tenderhearted, forgiving one another,**
> **even as God in Christ forgave you.**

> —EPHESIANS 4:32

Forgiveness is kind and tenderhearted. Forgiveness demonstrates love for others. We can lay down our judgment and walk away because Jesus laid down His life for us.

Blessings!

PRAYER: Ask God to show you where you are withholding forgiveness. Then ask Him for the peace and love to forgive.

SECTION 5:

LIVING PROTECTED

Everyone wants to feel safe and secure. Whether it be physically, mentally, or spiritually, feeling secure is very important. When we feel unsafe, we feel exposed, vulnerable, and even defenseless. No one wants to have those feelings.

Safety implies protection. When we feel safe physically, we feel shielded from anything that could physically harm us. Our mental safety is a bit more fragile. Mental and emotional security requires protecting our mental state from being attacked. It's the absence of fear and anxiety among other things.

So, what about our spiritual safety? I am not speaking about salvation but rather temptation. Spiritual safety is strongly linked to mental safety, because the most common tool of the enemy is doubt. If he can make us doubt, he can make us do.

The first example of temptation in the Bible is found in Genesis 3:1–7. Satan caused Eve to doubt what God had told them and then she did what she should not have done. She lowered her spiritual shield of faith just long enough for the enemy to plant a seed of doubt that grew to sin.

In this section, we will unpack more truths found in the model prayer and discover how our relationship with the Master helps us live protected, safe, and secure from the schemes of the devil. Shields up, ladies!

Blessings!

LESSON 17

Forever Follow

The preschool game "Follow the Leader" has simple rules. Children take turns leading and the other children follow, because that is the one rule of the game. They must follow. But that is not how great leaders lead.

What attributes make a great leader?

What attributes of God make Him someone you desire to follow?

> And do not lead us into temptation.
>
> —MATTHEW 6:13A

One cannot lead without someone following. This section of the model prayer implicitly affirms we intend to follow the Lord. When we make this request of our Master, "Do not lead me," we are proclaiming our dedication to follow Him wherever He leads. Our trust in Him is unwavering. We are submitted completely to His will.

We are not dictating where He should lead us, but respectfully requesting the easier path. Let's be real—we don't always get the easy path. Let's also be clear—God does not tempt us.

> **Let no one say when he is tempted, "I am tempted by God"; for God cannot be tempted by evil, nor does He Himself tempt anyone.**

> —JAMES 1:13

Matthew 4:13 calls Satan the tempter. He tempted Eve in the garden, and had the audacity to try tempting the Son of God. He has been slithering around tempting people ever since.

Temptation has three sources. It comes from Satan for sure. It also comes from the fallen world around us. We may not want to admit the last one, but temptation also originates in the flesh. We have a sin nature. We must deny the flesh, the world, and Satan to be able to successfully follow God in the opposite direction of temptation. We cannot walk parallel with temptation and be successful. We must turn and run the other way.

How then do we reconcile these truths? God does not tempt us, and yet Jesus taught us to pray for God to not lead us to temptation. Let's see how a few other translations interpret Matthew 6:13.

The Message (MSG): **Keep us safe from ourselves and the Devil.**

Good News Translation (GNB): **Do not bring us to hard testing,** but **keep us safe from the Evil One.**

New Living Translation (NLT): **And don't let us yield to temptation, but rescue us from the evil one.**

Now pair that with this verse.

> No temptation has overtaken you except such as is common to man; but God is faithful, who will not allow you to be tempted beyond what you are able, but with the temptation will also make the way of escape, that you may be able to bear it.

> —1 CORINTHIANS 10:13

It's comforting to see that temptation is common and God is faithful. Underline the words "will not allow" and "beyond" in the verse above. Let them sink in. This verse holds two very important promises: God cares enough to limit the temptation and also provides a way out. He desires our success. I hope this deepens your understanding of today's passage.

In the space below, describe what it means to ask God to "not lead us into temptation."

I love math. In my world, two negatives make a positive. "Do not" (negative) "lead us into temptation" (negative) translates into, "Do lead me to dedication and obedience" (positive). I am asking my Lord and Savior, who is faithful and works all together for my good and His glory, to light my path and I am committed to follow Him.

Sister, the voice of the tempter is alive and well. He will make every attempt to lead us off the path that God has for us. Our ability to focus on God's voice, recognize it, and follow Him away from that temptation grows as our relationship with Him grows deeper.

God does not tempt us, but He does reserve the right to test us. God's tests are intended to strengthen us. His goal is for us to learn what He is teaching so we can pass the test. His desire is our success. Temptation's goal is failure and it is not of God. See the difference?

> **Obedience to God always brings rewards – not the least of which is increased communication with God.**[1]

> —PRISCILLA SHIRER

Obedience to God's Word and following His will always leads us in the right direction and to the right action. When the enemy tries to divert us, we must run toward the Savior. Follow Him and He will either show us the way out or give us the strength to withstand the enemy.

Blessings!

PRAYER: Ask God to lead you to the next step on your journey with Him. Then follow, Sister!

LESSON 18

Forever Trust

What comes to your mind when you hear the word "deliver"? For me, it's a package. I order something and it magically arrives on my front porch a few days later. Without giving a great deal of thought, ordering online requires that we put trust in several things. We trust the provider to get the order right, charge the card correctly, package well, and ship quickly to the correct address. We must also trust that the carrier will deliver an undamaged package in a timely manner to the right place. We have probably experienced most, if not all, of these trusts being broken at some point. We know this system is flawed and we will be disappointed at times.

Isn't it refreshing to know God is perfect and will never let us down? His deliverance is always right on time.

> **And do not lead us into temptation,**
> **but deliver us from the evil one.**
>
> —MATTHEW 6:13

Although we never want to face the evil one, the reality is that we cannot grow to be the person God intends without facing and overcoming some temptations. If we are never challenged, we never grow. Our spiritual muscles grow and strengthen with use and challenges. When we trust God through these difficult times, our relationship with Him becomes so very intimate.

Maybe the best example in the Bible of a child of God facing the evil one is Job. Job faced many temptations to turn from God, but he never did. He stood strong in his faith. God ultimately rewarded him for his faithfulness.

Please read Job 1:12. God allowed Satan a wide berth in the life of Job, but there is one critical point I want to note in this passage. Satan was allowed power, but God has final authority. Sister, God may be allowing Satan a wide berth in our lives today, but never forget that God has ultimate authority. He will deliver us in His perfect timing.

It is easy to get discouraged in times of testing and temptation. Some trials grab hold of us and it seems they will never let us go.

Please read Mark 9:14–18 and answer the following questions.

Who needed deliverance?

Who tried to deliver him?

What was the result?

Jesus encountered a man whose son was demon-possessed. He had asked Jesus's disciples to cast out the demon, but they were unable to.

Now please read Mark 9:19–20.

What was the reaction of the spirit in the presence of Jesus?

Immediately the spirit reacted. Know this: Satan cannot stand in the presence of our Almighty God. James 2:19 tells us the demons believe and tremble. Bear with me a moment longer and see the end of this encounter.

Please read Mark 9:21–27.

What was the father's request of Jesus?

My translation puts it this way:

> **But if You can do anything, have compassion on us and help us.**
>
> —MARK 9:22B

If? He is speaking to Jesus and he says "if." I don't believe he is challenging Jesus's ability. On the contrary, it's a raw, passionate request from the heart of a tired, fearful father. His meaning was more likely "if you will." Can we admit for a moment that we all get to a place where we tell the Lord, "If You will"?

Jesus understood this father's meaning and I love His response.

> **Jesus said to him, "If you can believe, all things are possible to him who believes."**
>
> ——MARK 9:23

If we can dig deep and believe, then it's possible. Faith healed this child, and faith will make our deliverance possible as well, my friend.

> **Immediately the father of the child cried out and said with tears, "Lord, I believe; help my unbelief!"**
>
> ——MARK 9:24

Have you ever felt like this father? When it says he cried out, I believe that was literal. I can hear the tears in his strained voice as he begs, "Lord, I believe. Now please help my unbelief." It is so easy to let our struggles drag us down, but our Lord can even help our unbelief. When our faith wavers, we only need to grab hold of Him with all the strength we can muster and He will deliver us. He is able.

> I will love You, O Lord, my strength. the Lord is my rock and my fortress and my deliverer; my God, my strength, in whom I will trust; my shield and the horn of my salvation, my stronghold. I will call upon the Lord, who is worthy to be praised; so shall I be saved from my enemies.
>
> —PSALM 18:1–3

Please underline all the "I will" statements in these verses.

When I am willing to live in His will, the Lord becomes my rock, my fortress, my deliverer, my strength, my shield, my salvation, my stronghold. I will be saved from my enemies, even the evil one. I will praise Him for He alone is worthy.

Blessings!

PRAYER: Call upon the Lord today. Let Psalm 18:1–3 be your prayer.

SECTION 6:

LIVING TO GLORIFY

Our journey together is almost over. Few things last forever, yet in the New King James Version we find 400 occurrences of the word. In the Book of Psalms alone, we find the word "forever" used 138 times. Unlike things of this world that wither and fade, our God is eternal, and His kingdom is forever.

The LORD shall endure forever - **PSALM 9:7**

His name shall endure forever - **PSALM 72:17**

The Lord is King forever - **PSALM 10:16**

He rules by His power forever - **PSALM 66:7**

His mercy endures forever - **34 occurrences in PSALMS**

His righteousness endures forever - **PSALM 111:3**

The truth of the Lord endures forever - **PSALM 117:2**

The Lord shall reign forever - **PSALM 146:10**

For these reasons, and so many more, we live to glorify His name. This section will wrap up our study, but I pray that we live out this verse the rest of our days.

> **I will praise You, O Lord my God, with all my heart, and I will glorify Your name forevermore.**

> — PSALM 86:12

Blessings!

LESSON 19

Forever Praise

Have you ever been in a praise and worship service where the hair on the back of your neck stands up because the message of the song is so impactful? Or listening to a song on the radio driving down the road and tears fill your eyes because the words touch your heart so tenderly? When we know our God and Savior intimately and our relationship is strong, our praise becomes sweet and tender.

Jesus chose to end His model prayer with reverent affirmation of who God is. God certainly doesn't need our affirmation, but it is sweet praise when we acknowledge that He is our King, all powerful and deserving of glory.

> **For Yours is the kingdom and the power and the glory forever.**
>
> —MATTHEW 6:13C

We discussed God's kingdom in Lesson 5. Jesus is not being repetitious, but acknowledging what the Scriptures tell us about our God.

Please look up the following verses and write beside them who they say God is.

Genesis 14:20	

Psalm 47:7	
1 Timothy 6:15	(3 can be found here)
Psalm 10:16	

Yours is the kingdom, God. We praise You, our King, forever. Amen!

We praise God not only as our King but as our all-powerful God.

Please do the same with the following verses. How is God described?

Revelation 4:8	
Isaiah 10:21	
Psalm 99:8	

Psalm 18:46	

We praise our Almighty God for He is all powerful. He is our Mighty God. He is the God of mercy and forgiveness, and He is the God of our salvation.

Now record who God is according to these verses.

Psalm 24:7	
Romans 15:13	
2 Corinthians 13:11	

We praise the King of Glory! The God of hope, love, and peace! Praise His name! And what happens if we don't? Let's check in with Jesus as He triumphantly entered Jerusalem.

> Then, as He was now drawing near the descent of the Mount of Olives, the whole multitude of the disciples began to rejoice and praise God with a loud voice for all the mighty works they had seen, saying:
>
> "Blessed is the King who comes in the name of the Lord! Peace in heaven and glory in the highest!"

And some of the Pharisees called to Him from the crowd, "Teacher, rebuke Your disciples."

But He answered and said to them, "I tell you that if these should keep silent, the stones would immediately cry out."

—LUKE 19:37–40

I don't know about you, but I *am not* going to let a rock out-praise me! He is the King of Glory, and I will praise His name forever and ever.

Blessings!

PRAYER: Praise His name. Tell Him who He is to you.

LESSON 20

Forever Follow-Through

We began this study with the disciples witnessing Jesus speak with His Father. They desired the same intimacy, the same relationship, with God that Jesus had. We have covered many aspects of our relationship with the Father. Now I have a piercing question.

Who sees your relationship with the Father and desires the same?

The truth is, we can gain all the knowledge humanly possible and still fall short of an intimate relationship with God. Relationship is not a fact; it comes by following through. It is a fact that I love my family. But if I never act on that love, they will never know the depth of it.

The last word of the model prayer . . .

Amen.

—MATTHEW 6:13D

Amen, simply put, means "so be it." We have come before our heavenly Father expressing our relationship with Him, our submission to Him, and our faith in provision from Him. We have requested forgiveness based on our ability to forgive. We have claimed protection under the shelter of His mighty wings. And now we glorify Him with praise and commitment to action.

Kay Arthur gives us this insight into glory:

> In the Hebrew language it means "to give the correct opinion or estimate of." . . . Can you see how awesome it is to know that you have been created for God's glory? That you are to live in such a way as to give all of creation a correct opinion or estimate of who God is? What does that mean to you, O child of God, who is called by His name?[1]

Take a moment to answer Kay's question. What does that mean to you?

If you feel that you are not living up to this, you are not alone. Don't be discouraged! It takes thirty days to make or break a habit. I challenge you to commit to being "all in" for God by glorifying Him daily for one month. I believe it will change your life.

Are you up for that commitment? If so, please sign your name here.

Let's take a moment to record a few things that we can refer to over the next thirty days.

Please read Galatians 5:22–23 and list the fruit of the Spirit in the left column below.

Fruit	Start	Week 1	Week 2	Week 3	Week 4

I love a good chart! This one is simple. It helps us track our progress toward giving a correct opinion of God to the world around us. We must live intentionally to progress. We must know where we are starting and where we want to go.

In the "Start" column of the chart, rate yourself on how well you bear each fruit right now. Use a scale of 1 to 10 where 1 is not at all and 10 is consistently.

We may already have a great head start. These are the fruits of the Holy Spirit. And Who lives within us? The Holy Spirit! As we allow Him dominant control and influence in every part of our lives, we will bear more and more fruit.

Use the last four columns to evaluate and record your progress over the coming weeks.

I hate to go there, but it's like losing weight. If we never step on the scale, we have no incentive to stay with it. We must "step on the scale" weekly to remind ourselves where we are and what our goal is.

I encourage you to follow through with all that you know about God in your relationship with Him. Lean into His goodness.

Draw near to God and He will draw near to you.

—JAMES 4:8A

In conclusion, I encourage you to tell your story. You never know how your relationship with God may inspire someone else and help their relationship with Him grow.

Write the name of someone you can share your story of God's goodness with this week.

Sister, it has been my honor to study God's word with you. It is my prayer that this study has helped you draw nearer to our Lord. I find it very fitting that we end our study with the last verse of God's Word to us.

The grace of our Lord Jesus Christ be with you all. Amen.

—REVELATION 22:21

Blessings, my sister!

PRAYER: Ask God to give you the desire to follow through on all that He has for you. Amen.

Note: If you are serious about the 30-day commitment, there is a larger copy of the chart on pages 114-115. You can cut out and post it in a place you will see each day, like your mirror or refrigerator.

Grace to you and peace
from God our Father and
the Lord Jesus Christ.

—EPHESIANS 1:2

ABOUT THE AUTHOR

LYNN WISE is an IT professional with a passion for women's ministry. She is a Bible teacher and an author of five Bible studies and is active in women's ministry in her local church.

She wrote and taught her first Bible study, based on Psalm 24, in 2014. Since then, she has been writing and teaching Bible studies as the Lord leads. Her primary motivation is to help women draw closer to one another and to Christ as they study and apply God's Word to their everyday lives.

Lynn lives in New Albany, Mississippi. She is a member of Hillcrest Baptist Church, also in New Albany. Her daughter Jessica and son-in-law Rob live nearby. They have blessed her with three beautiful grandchildren, Fisher, Olivia Hart, and Cooper, who affectionately know her as "BumBum."

NOTES

Section 1

1. Oswald Chambers, *If You Will Ask: Reflections of the Power of Prayer*, Updated Language Edition (Grand Rapids, MI: Discovery House, 2012), 50.

Section 2

1. Warren W. Wiersbe, *The Wiersbe Bible Commentary, New Testament* (Colorado Springs: David C. Cook, 2007), 173.

Lesson 6

1. William G. Smith, *The Oxford Dictionary of English Proverbs* (London: Oxford University Press, 1949), 582.
2. George Herbert, *Jacula Prudentum: Outlandish Proverbs, Sentences, etc.* (London: The Castle in Cornhill, 1640), 68.

Lesson 9

1. Warren W. Wiersbe, *The Wiersbe Bible Commentary, New Testament* (Colorado Springs, CO: David C. Cook, 2007), 752.

Section 4

1. C. S. Lewis, *The Weight of Glory* (New York, NY: Simon & Schuster, 1996), 135.

Lesson 11

1. Michel de Montaigne, quoted in Don Joseph Goewey, "85 Percent of What We Worry About Never Happens." Last updated December

6, 2017. *Huffpost*: *www.huffpost.com/entry/85-of-what-we-worry-about_b_8028368* (April 21, 2020).

2. Don Joseph Goewey, "85 Percent of What We Worry About Never Happens." Last updated December 6, 2017. *Huffpost*: *www.huffpost.com/entry/85-of-what-we-worry-about_b_*8028368 (April 21, 2020).

Lesson 16

1. George Herbert, *QuoteActions*: *www.quoteactions.com/a/share/1416/1140* (August 25, 2020).

Lesson 17

1. Priscilla Shirer, *He Speaks to Me: Preparing to Hear the Voice of God* (Chicago: Moody Publishers, 2006), 187.

Lesson 20

1. Kay Arthur, *Lord, I Want to Know You: A Devotional Study of the Names of God* (New York: Waterbrook Press, 1992, 2000), 12.

Fruitful Journey

Fruit	Start	Week 1	Week 2	Week 3	Week 4

Want to keep going?

Fruit	Start	Week 1	Week 2	Week 3	Week 4

Made in the USA
Columbia, SC
10 January 2022

52973435R00071